INDHOLD

Before we drive into what Azure DevOps is, let us first look at what DevOps is. DevOps is not some fancy term that Microsoft has created; it is a term created back in 2009 where the idea was to break down the barriers between Development and Operations in the hope of speeding up the deployment cycle by shortening the time from development to production. To accomplish this, one of the critical points of DevOps is Continuous integration and continuous delivery (CI/CD). (CI/CD) means that you are encouraged to create many small releases, the idea behind this is that you should break all your tasks down so you can release them to production with no to minimal visible changes to the end customers.

An example could be that you could release some functions to the production environment without it being used anywhere, but why would you want to release code that is not yet being used, well the reason is that it will let your unit tests test the code in a production environment, without having to risk an end user running into untested code, and furthermore when making small releases you will also make it easier to identify any "bad" code and speeding up the process of rolling a release back. How many times have you tried to release a large amount of code, crossing your fingers that everything has been tested because doing a rollback is next to impossible? To be able to implement CI/CD effetely, you will need to be able to automize as much as possible, and this means writing unit tests, creating automatic builds, automatic releases, and having infrastructure as code. Another strength point for small releases is that it is easier for operations to approve many minor changes rather than one large one, which means it will make it easier for the team to deliver on time. To set up an efficient CI/CD pipeline, you must make sure that every person in your team knows what their job is and have the tools needed to perform their work. The most common thing that gets in the way of having a smooth pipeline are bottlenecks. A bottleneck can occur if you, for example, have seven developers and only one tester; in this scenario, then the tester will not be able to test new features fast enough, leaving the developers wasting time in a waiting position. The other example could be that you have one developer and five testers, this again will leave the testers waiting for the developer to finish their code so that the tester can test it. If you have a bottleneck, it is crucial to find it and fix the problem at the source, meaning that fixing anything before or after the bottleneck is useless.

DevOps was in short created to break down the old silo structure where each team would be put into their own silo, where you, for example, would have a silo for development, a silo for operations, and a silo for project management. Instead, DevOps encourage you to let your organization be more fluent and breaking down the "wall of confusion" which is where all teams try to deliver their products by throwing it over the wall.

So, the flow in DevOps would be Plan->Code->Build->Test->Release->Deploy->Operate->Monitor

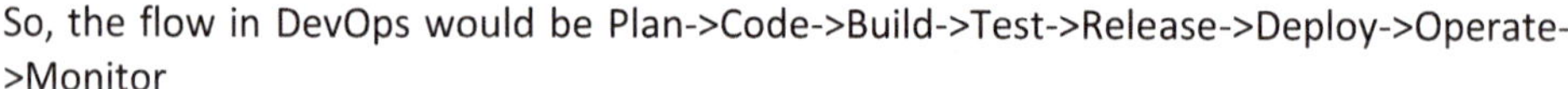

One of the cornerstones in DevOps is complete transparency, which is achieved through open dialog and the ability to understand the other team member's challenges. The right-hand needs to know what the left hand is doing and vice versa. One of the ways that DevOps encourages transparency is by using the practice of A Day In My Shoes which simply put means, that one day a month a developer, will follow a person from operation around seeing how their day is, and what problems they are facing on a day-to-day basis, and vice versa, a person from operations follows a developer around for a day.

Key points in DevOps

Dark Releases: The idea behind dark releases is that you release, code to production without letting it be publicly available, but only allowing a limited number of users use the code, allowing these users to test the code in production, and once tested making it publicly available by toggling a setup field. Dark Releases can also be used to allow developers to push code to production that might not be 100% ready. Still, by encapsulating the code, it can safely be put into production, allowing for small releases.

10 Releases a day: DevOps encourages CI/CD to the extreme, by having the ten releases a day strategy, what this means is that you should always be pushing code to production, and by setting a goal for ten releases a day, you will naturally end up with tiny releases.

Agile Development: DevOps highly recommends teams to use agile development; in the coding phase, agile development is designed to handle short release cycles.

Team: Any DevOps team should contain the following roles; Product Owner, Tester (QA), Developer and Operations (infrastructure)

Source control: Source control is necessary when it comes to DevOps, and not only application code should be in source control, but everything including scripts which are used to set up servers and services and documentation.

Automation: When everything is in source control, it should be easy to automate, creating tests, and developer environments. All code tests should also be able to run automatic, including Unit tests, integration tests, UI tests, and load tests.

Environments: In DevOps, it should be possible to spin up a development or test environment that matches the production environment (excluding data) within minutes.

Infrastructure as code: All infrastructure should be written as code, like PowerShell scripts, so you easily can create a new environment anywhere within minutes.

There is much more to DevOps than what I have written. However, I will leave you to explore the rest on your own. ☺

Azure DevOps is the current version of Microsoft's old Team Foundation Server. Azure DevOps is a set of tools that can help you quickly implement DevOps in your projects by providing you with everything you need from project management to source control to testing and CI/CD. In many ways, you can view Azure DevOps as your one-stop tool for any project. But of course, like anything Microsoft, nothing is free. However, Microsoft does allow you to have up to 5 full users for free plus an infinite amount of MSDN users, besides the full users, you can also have as many stakeholders as you want.

Full users:

These users can be assigned any roles and given any permission sets that you wish.

Stakeholders:

The stakeholders are limited users that can only. Sign into a project, Add a work item, View the product backlog and add new work to it, View work in progress on the Kanban board and Find work assigned to them or query for other work items. The wonderful thing about stakeholders is that they are free, and even though they are limited in access, for the most part, both consultants and product owners should be able to manage with only a stakeholder-user.

TIP: Microsoft uses Azure DevOps to maintain its products, including Windows and Office, meaning that they take their own medicine when it comes to stability and features.

To get started with Azure DevOps, you must first create an account; you can do this by going to https://azure.microsoft.com/en-us/services/devops/?nav=min this will in turn also create your first organization.

CREATING AN ORGANIZATION

When creating an organization, you will have to choose its location and choose a unique name, which will also be your direct URL going forward.

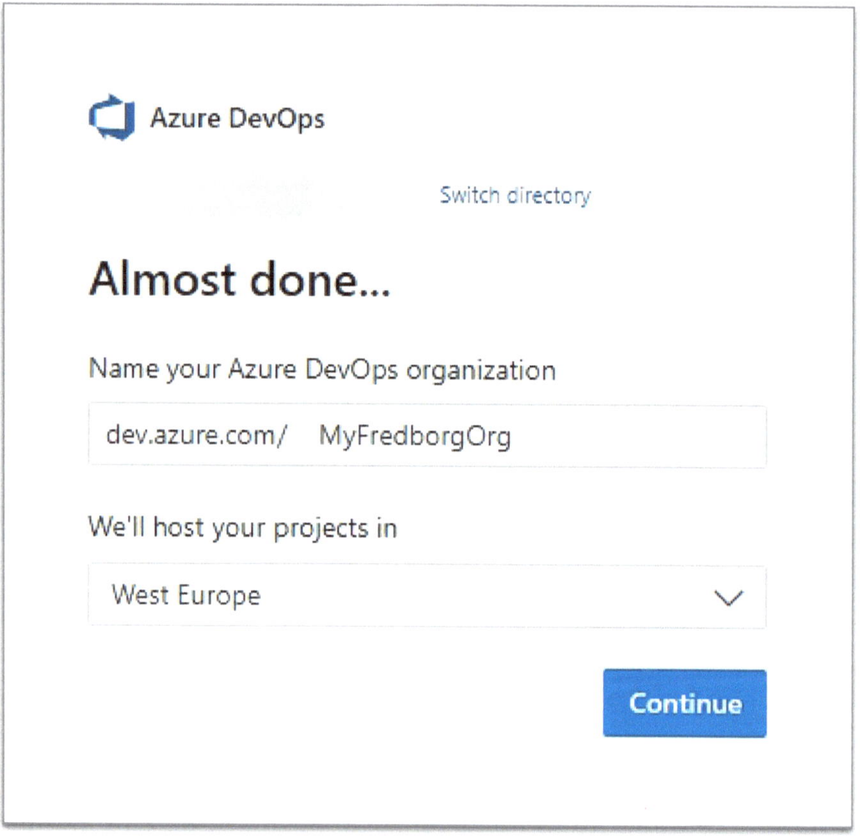

You can create as many organizations as you want, and this will take us to the next step, which is creating a project because, without a project, your organization is an empty shell. To create a project, you must first give it a project name and choose whether you want the project to be public or private. In most cases, you would select a private project unless you are working on an open-source project; however, should you choose a public project, it will open up for some free features that you would have to pay for in a private project. One of the main advantages is that you will get unlimited free build minutes on your pipelines using a public project.

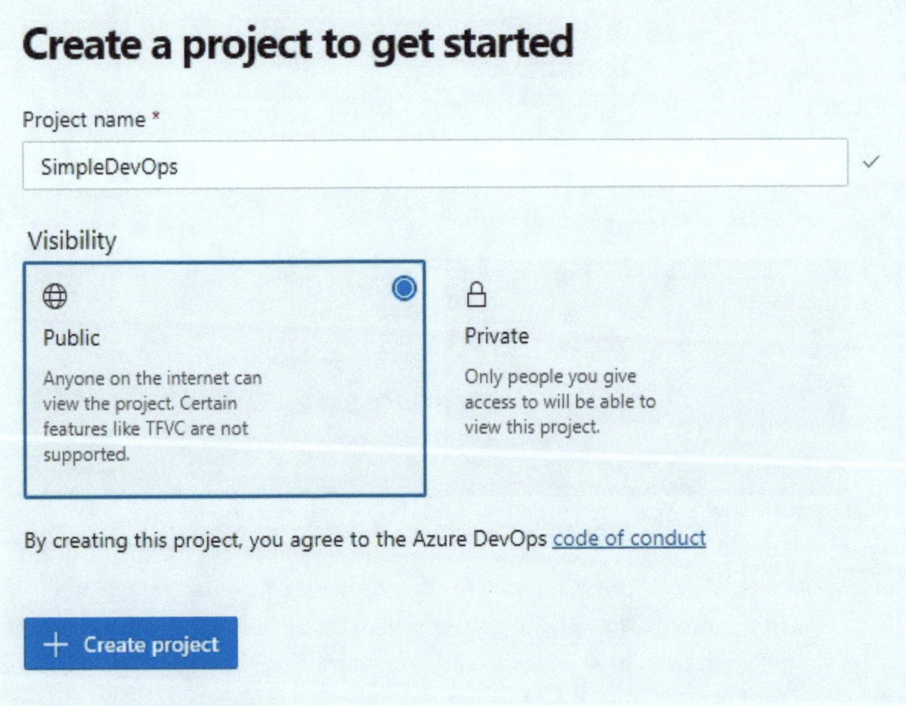

Once you press **create project,** it will take you to your newly created project; your first project will automatically choose to run Basic Process, when you create your next project, you will be able to choose both which process it should run and what you wish to use for version control.

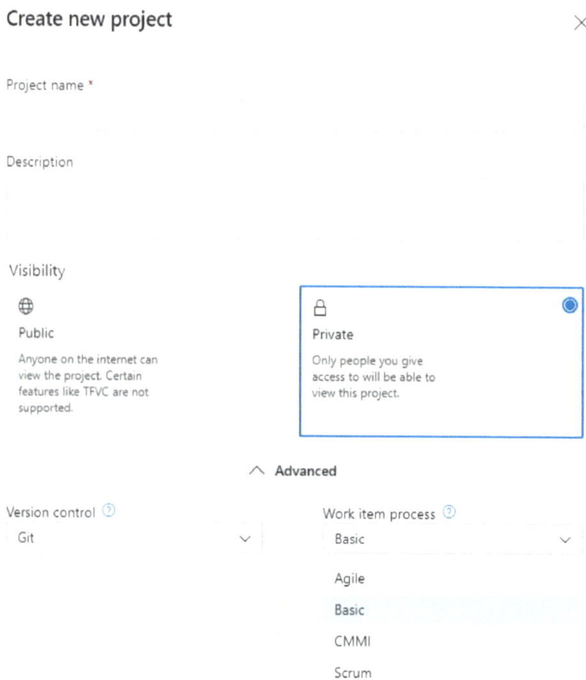

We will get back to process in a little while, and how you can create your own. You can have an unlimited number of projects for any given organization, so the structure of Azure DevOps is, you can have X number of organizations. Under each organization, you can X number of projects. Now, this might seem very "so what?" but it is quite powerful, the reason being that you have global settings for your organization, and you have local settings for your projects, which means that you can customize your projects, so they fit your requirements.

ORGANIZATION SETTINGS

When you go to your organization's landing page, you will see in the bottom left a link called **Organization Settings** when you press this link you will be taken to a page where you have a list of settings for your organization.

The first page that you will see is the Overview

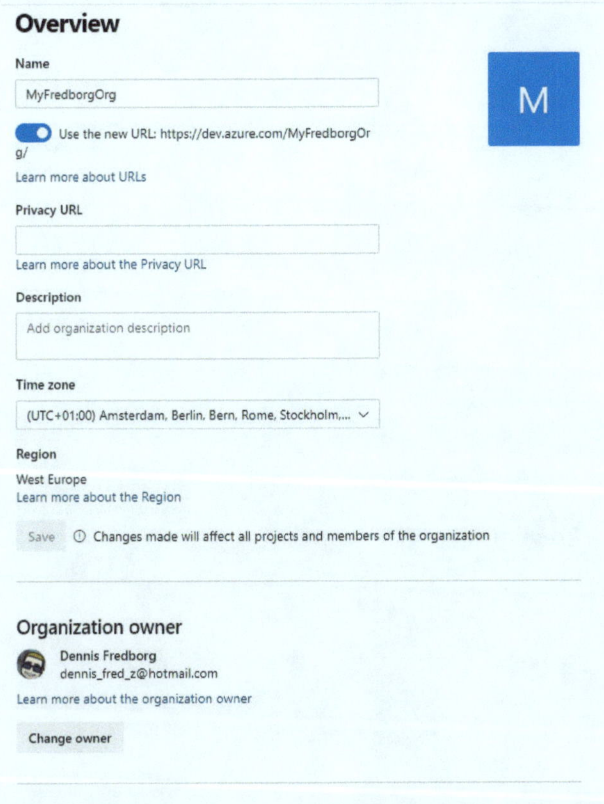

Delete organization

On this page, you will be able to change the name of your organization, the time zone, add a description, change the owner of your organization, and delete the organization. The pages of interest are the following.

Projects: This page lists all your projects and lets you create a new project, delete a project, or rename a project.

Users: This page will let you manage your users, it also gives you the possibility to create new users, where you can define their access level (Basic, Stakeholder, Visual Studio Subscriber), and which projects they should have access to. If you are part of a larger team, you can create groups so that you can control permissions on a group level instead of on a user level.

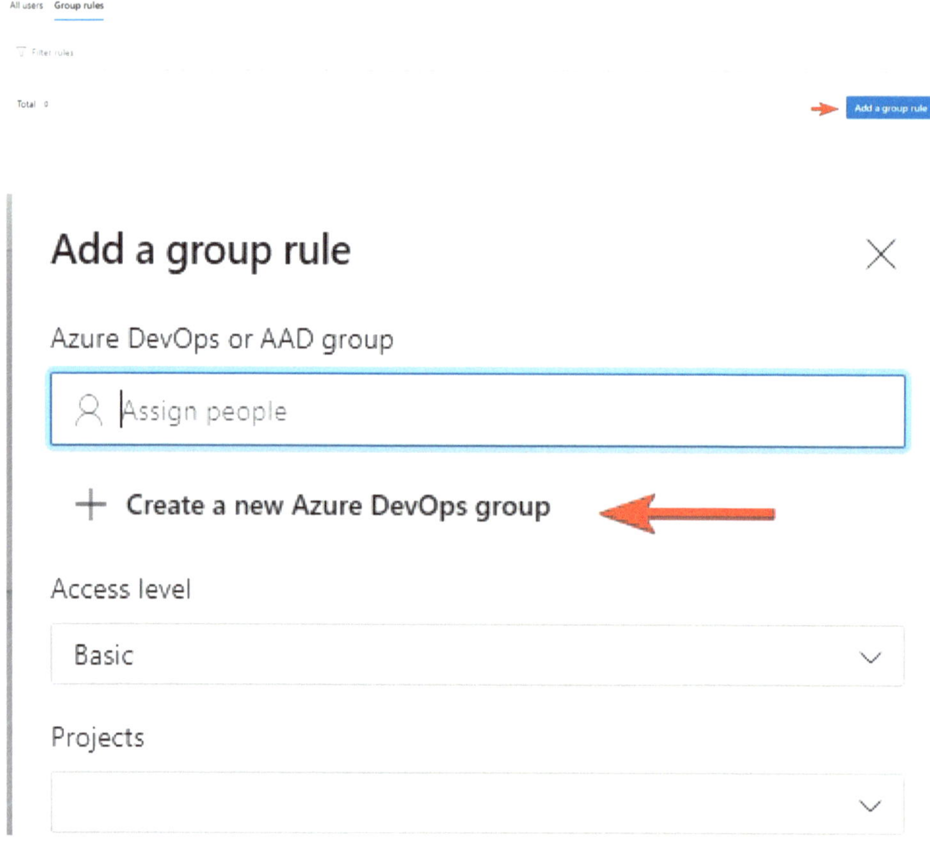

Billing: This will show you what plan you are using and what you can upgrade to.

Auditing: Gives you the possibility to view and download a log of what is going on in your DevOps.

Notifications: Here, you can control what kind of notifications are being sent and to whom.

Extensions: Gives an overview of what extensions are installed, and if someone has requested a given extension to be installed. You can install extensions from the marketplace, but we will get back to that later.

Process: This is where you can view and create your own processes. To create your own process, you must create an inherited process.

Where you then give it a name and a description.

Create inherited process from Agile

Create a new inherited process to enable customizations.

Agile [system process]

MyAgileProcess

Description

This is my new process

Learn more

Create process **Cancel**

Once it is created, you can click on the newly created process, and it will allow you to customize your process where you can create your own work item types or removing some of the existing. You can also customize any work item types by clicking on it. There are three tabs; the layout tab, which will let you add new fields and remove fields.

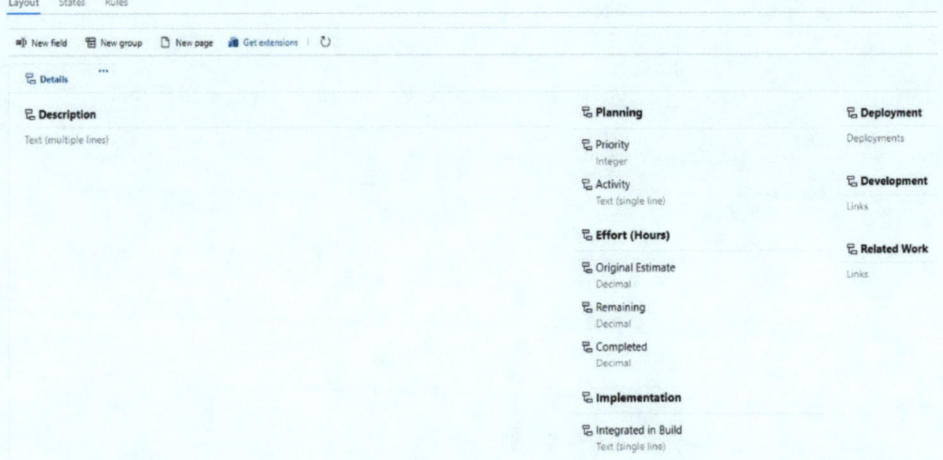

States which will let you control which states your work item can have.

For each work item type, you can customize the workflow to support y

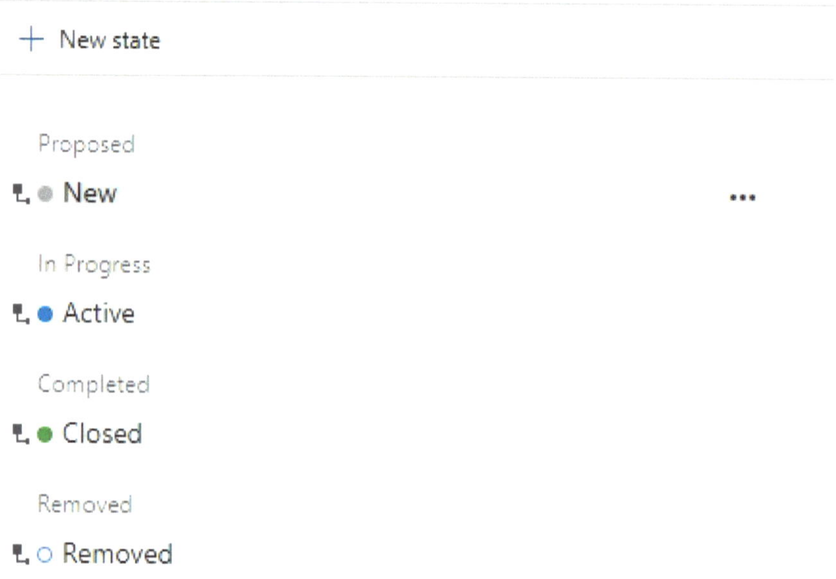

Rules will let you create rules for your work items, which is very powerful because this can help you to automate a lot of your workflow, an example could be that on work item create, it should automatically assign the work item to someone.

⚡ New work item rule

A rule allows you to specify actions on work item fields to automate their behavior. By defining conditions system applies these changes to the fields. Learn more about work item rules ⤢

Name | Assign User | *

Conditions ⓘ

When   [⊞ A work item is created … ⌄]

+ New condition

Actions ⓘ

Then   [☺ Use the current user to set the value of … ⌄]   [Assigned To ⌄]

+ New action

[Save]   [Cancel]

You could also create a flow where once the developer changes the state of the work item to test, it would automatically assign the task to a tester.

Once you have set up the work items that you wish to use in your process and the flows, you can start using it in your projects, giving you a tailored experience.

Agent pools: This will let you manage your agent pools, agent pools are used to maintain your azure agents, if you click on an agent pool, you will get an overview of which jobs has been executed in the given pool, you will also be able to create a new agent or update all your agents, we will get back to agents when we get to Azure pipelines.

There are more settings you can play around with, but these are the ones that I feel are most relevant.

Like organizations, you can set up your project in different ways, to get to the project settings you must go to the project that you wish to customize and press the **Project Settings** link. The first page is the overview, where you can change the name of your project, add a description, change the icon, and visibility. You can also view the project administrators and add new ones, you can delete the project, and you can manage which services you wish to use in your project. Besides the **Overview** page, the following pages might be of interest.

Teams: Here, you can see which teams can access your project.

Permissions: Lets you control and create permission sets, giving you an effortless way to control who can do what.

Notifications: Lets you control who should be notified and when.

Service Hooks: Here you can set up hooks, that will automatically notify a third party when something specific happens in your project, there is a lot of build-in products like teams and app center, but you also have the ability to create webhooks which means you can integrate to any system. A simple example could be, when you create a new task, the system will call a third-party API, which would create a task in their system; this would, in turn, mean that you could keep two systems in sync. Another use case could be that once you complete a task, it would call an API with the number of hours spend on the task, which would then automatically be added to a time registration system.

Dashboards: This will let you set up what your team members are allowed to do with dashboards, whether they are allowed to create their own dashboards, delete or edit dashboards. We will get back to dashboards later.

Project configuration: Here you can setup Iterations with start and end dates, iterations are used for time boxing of your sprints, you can also create more areas allowing you to have more products in the same project.

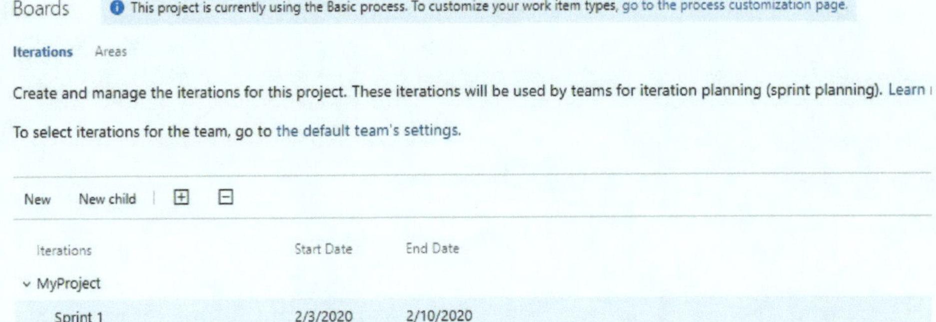

Team Configuration: This page consists of four parts where two of them are of interest, the first being the general; this will let you control which days your team is going to be working, which will be used when you set up your capacity and burndowns. The second is templates; these are used to pre-fill fields; it could, for example, be that you would like to use, user stores as your description on your tasks so you could set it up something like this.

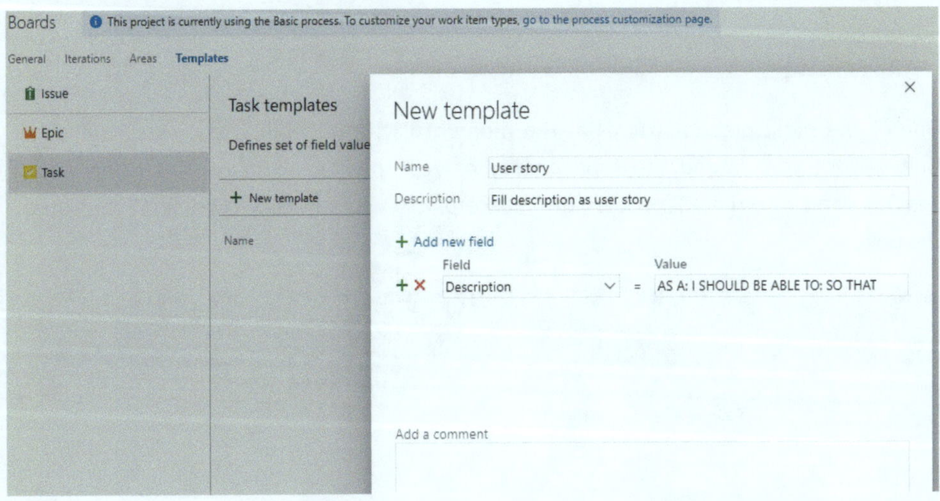

Repositories: Here you can set up how you wish your Repositories to work, one of the things that I would recommend if you are working in a team, is to lock down your master branch so that the only way that code can be added to the master branch is by completing a pull request, and thereby enforcing code review, to do this; go to your master branch and go to polices.

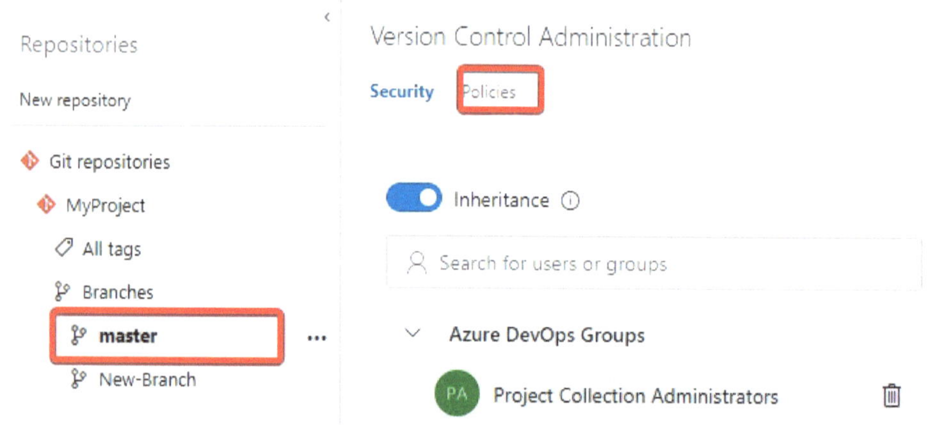

And then, setup Require a minimum number of reviewers and set it to any quantity that you find suitable, and press save.

These where the menu items that I felt are worth highlighting, thereby not saying that the rest does not contain things that are worth knowing. ⬚

MARKETPLACE

One of the most popular trends at the moment is the possibility to create extensions that will let you extend the functionality of your product, and on this front, Azure DevOps is no different. To access the marketplace, you can click the link at the top of the page.

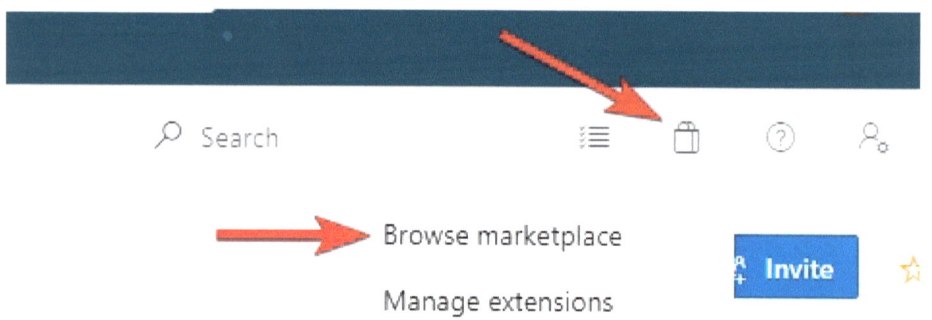

And choose browse marketplace, this will take you to the marketplace that works like any other app store, where you can view and install the extensions that you wish to use. I will highly recommend that you take a look at all the extensions since there are many great extensions that can help you in getting the experience that you want.

DASHBOARDS

Dashboards are used to give the user a quick overview of how your project is going, to create a dashboard go to Overview->Dashboards, and either create your own personal dashboard or edit the Teams dashboard.

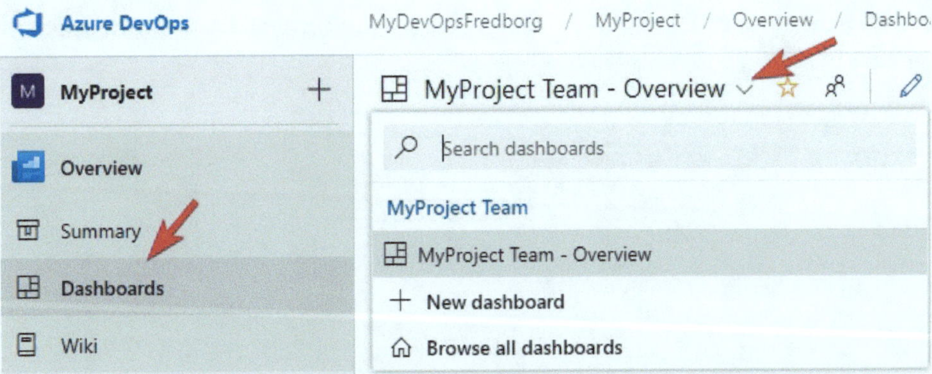

When creating a new dashboard, you have the ability to decide; whether it is a team or a project dashboard and whether you want it to refresh automatically. A dashboard is build up using widgets to get started press the Edit link, which will take you to a grid view.

In the left you will see a list of available widgets, extensions can expand this list, try adding the widget called Assigned to Me, this will add a new tile to your dashboard. If you click the settings icon on the widget, it will let you customize the widget, which in the case of Assigned to me is only the size.

Work assigned to Dennis Fredborg

While the code tile has a little bit more of set up, where you can set up which branch that you wish to monitor, should any of the other titles not give you what you want, you can use the Query Results and Query Title. Queries is a powerful tool that lets you build and do actions using a simple language.

WIKI

The wiki page is pretty much what you expect, it is a place where you can store any information that the team finds relevant for your project, and it works like any other wiki. Where you can create pages and add text and images, now it might sound like I am not impressed by the Wiki, but do not get me wrong using a Wiki correctly can make or break a project, because it is a great way to outline rules and roles for your project. It is a great place to store information that everyone should know.

SUMMARY

To summarize, you can create as many organizations as you wish, and under these organizations, you can added projects. Both organizations and projects can be customized to fit pretty much any type of workflow. You can create dashboards that can help your team always be up to date on what is going on in the project, and lastly, you can add wikis to your projects, again helping your team always to have the information that they need.

BOARDS

Boards are the place where most of you will spend most of your time in Azure DevOps. Boards are where all your project management will happen, and where all your tasks will be stored.

WORK ITEMS

Work Items are where you will have an overview of all the tasks in a project, and where you will create and delete new ones. To create a new work item, click the button Create Work Item, which will give you a drop-down of all available work item types for your project.

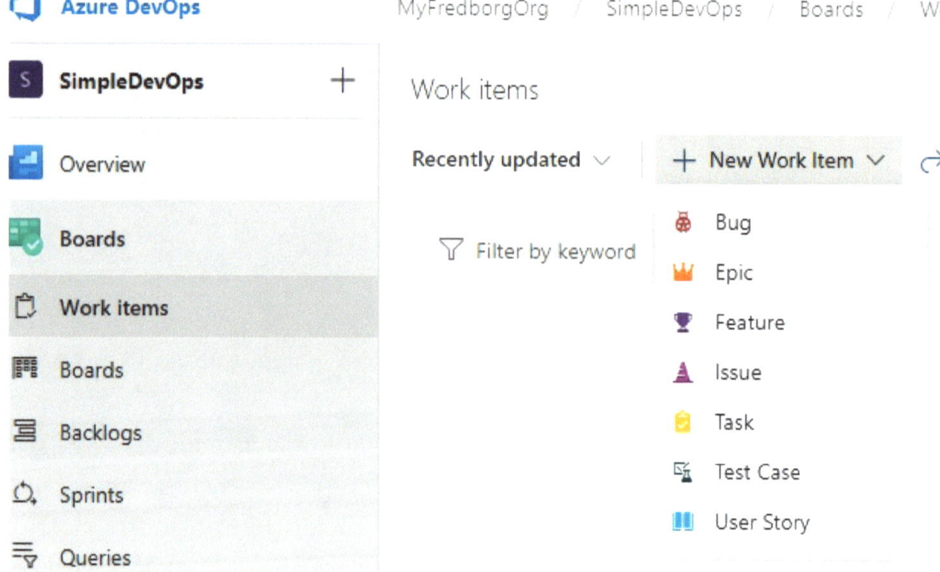

Remember that you can change which types should be available in your organization settings. To change, a process for your project go to Organization settings, click on the process, click on projects, click the three dots, and change process.

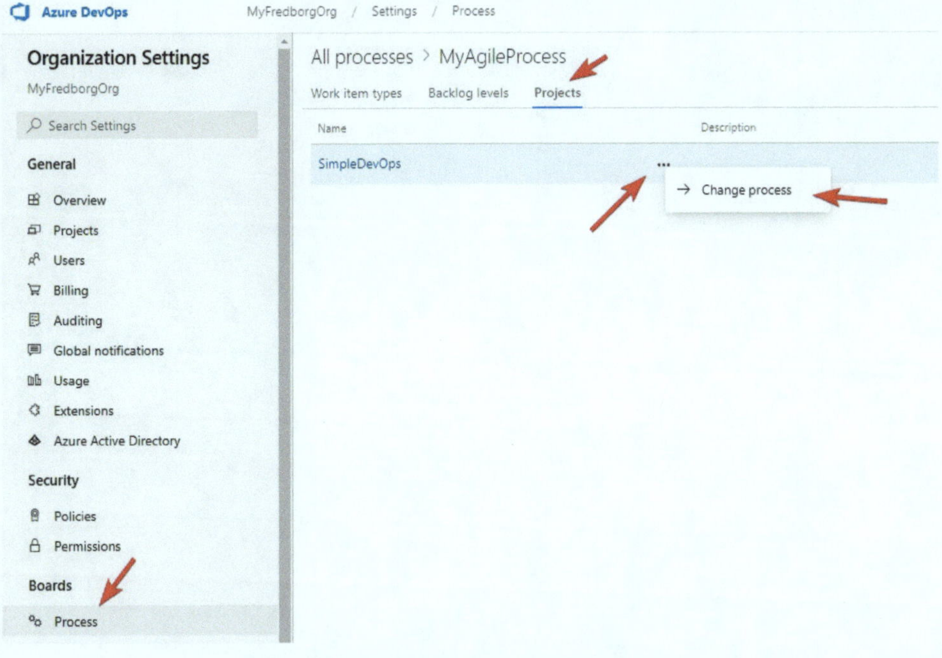

On all work items, you can create comments, give the work item a title, assign a responsible user, add it to an Area, add it to an iteration, estimate and provide it with story points.

You can create your own task types and use the existing in any way that you wish; however, I will try to give you a rundown of how I like to use the most common once.

Bug: If your project is running in the production or beta stage, then most likely, most of the work items that you are going to be seeing are bugs. Bugs are structured in such a way that it has two main parts Repro Steps, which is where the user will explain step by step how to reproduce the bug, and System information, which is where the user will enter information about their system.

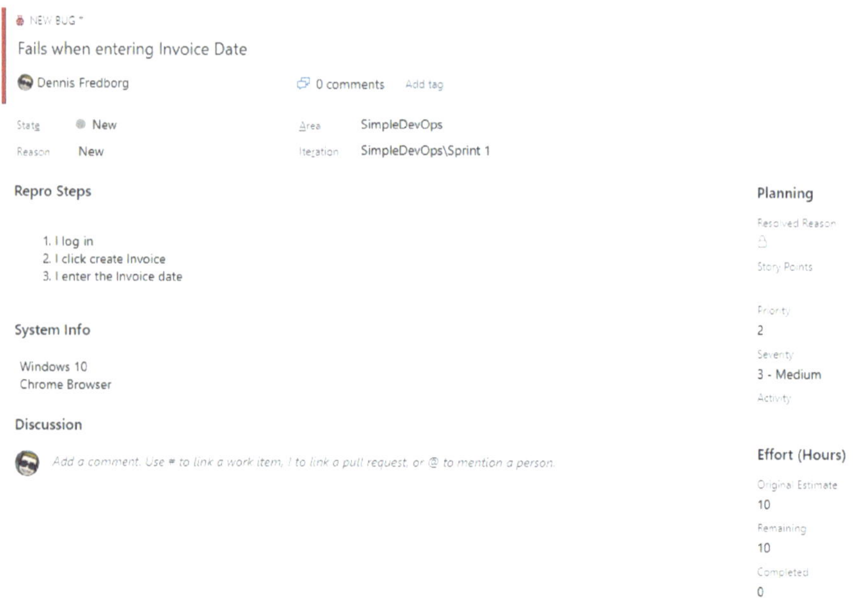

If your project is a web-based project, you can let your users use the Azure DevOps browser plugin to report bugs and tasks. What this plugin does is that it allows the users to record their experience, and automatically adds it to your work items.

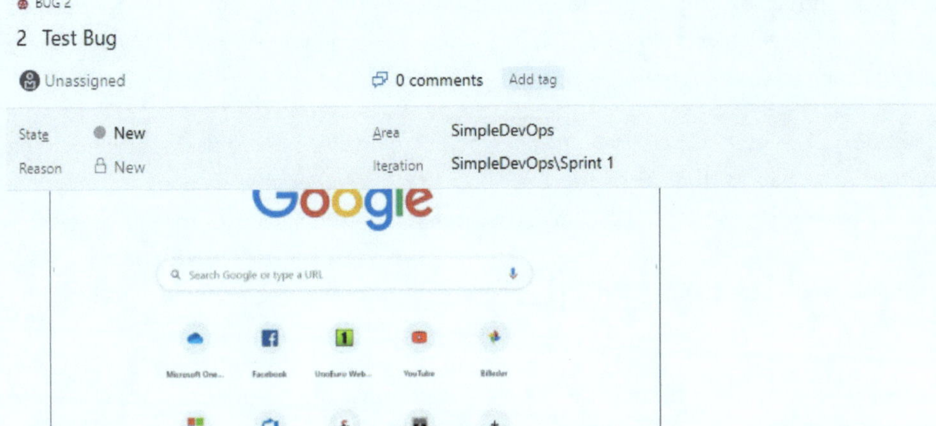

System Info

Browser - Name	Google Chrome 79
Browser - Language	da
Browser - Height	1056
Browser - Width	1936
Browser - UserAgent	Mozilla/5.0 (Windows NT 10.0; Win64; x64) AppleWebKit/537.36 (KHTML, like Gecko) Chrome/79.0.3945.130 Safari/537.36

We will get back to this great plugin when we are going to talk about tests.

Epic: Epics are typically used to describe tasks that are too large to fit in one user story; this means that an epic can contain many user stories. Epics can go across many iterations, you would typically never assign an epic to any given iteration, but instead, assign the user stories in the epic. You can view epics as their own backlog.

Feature: A feature is much like an epic, only on a smaller scale because where an epic is very broad, then a feature is cooked down to a single feature, but like the epic, then a feature consists of many small user stories.

Issue: The issue work item is used to keep track of any obstacles that might be in the way of the team completing their work; it could be something as simple as new batteries for your mouse, or a more significant obstacle like the build server needs more disk space.

Tasks: Tasks are the bread and butter of your projects; all work items should contain at least one task, which is where everything is broken down into as small and isolated pieces as possible. You could, for example, have a task to your user story called development, which you would assign to the developer and a task called QA, which you would assign to your QA team.

User Story: The user story is your entrance point to the customer, a user story should be written in a way so that both the user and the developer understands it, and they should be kept as simple as possible. This can be accomplished using the user story format. AS A ... I SHOULD BE ABLE TO... SO THAT. Also, a user story should always contain an acceptance criteria; here, I would recommend using the GIVEN...WHEN...THEN syntax to keep it simple.

As I wrote earlier, then there is no one right way to use your work items, so it is up to you to find the way that works best for your team and project.

BOARDS

Out of the box, Azure DevOps has set up a Kanban board for you, which is also one of the most used board types in DevOps, because of its speedy and straightforward release cycle. In Kanban, you must never have more than five active tasks in any given state. This is meant to provide you with a constant flow of releases because once your teams have started five tasks, you cannot begin anymore. Once the task is resolved, you must release it to production as fast as possible because you cannot have more than five tasks that are resolved but not released. The Kanban board was created by Toyota as part of their lean workflow and has proven to be an effetely way to keep your pipelines running. Now, like all things in Azure DevOps, then you can change the workflow of your Kanban boards, to do this click the configure action.

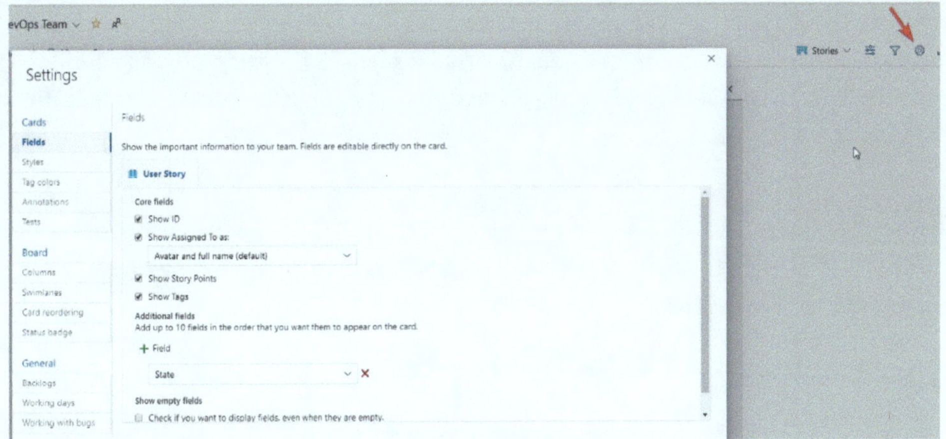

Where the first part under Cards is mostly about how you wish your board to look, in columns, you can add new columns and setting limits of how many tasks there is allowed in any given column.

BACKLOGS

If you wish to use SCRUM instead of Kanban, then backlogs are the way to go. A backlog is where you can get an overview of all your sprints, and where you can create new sprints. Backlogs and Sprints are terms used in SCRUM, where a backlog is a place where all your Work Items live until they are assigned to a sprint. A sprint is a time-boxed period of time, in which you must complete a set number of tasks, once a task is assigned to a sprint, it should never be taken out of that sprint. This also means that it is essential that you enter the correct capacity of your sprints, and you also estimate all your tasks, so it is easier for the project manager to get an overview of what is possible. To set the capacity of your sprint, go to the sprint menu and click capacity, and add the team members for that sprint.

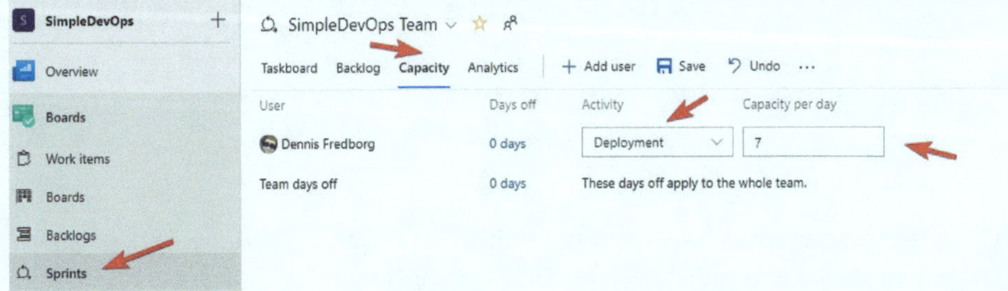

The cool thing about the capacity is that you are also able to factor in if your team members have days off both individually or as a team. So, setting up your backlogs correctly is a powerful tool for your project managers and stakeholders to see the progress of your projects.

QUERIES

You can use queries to create the views that you wish. To create a new query, go to queries and click New Query.

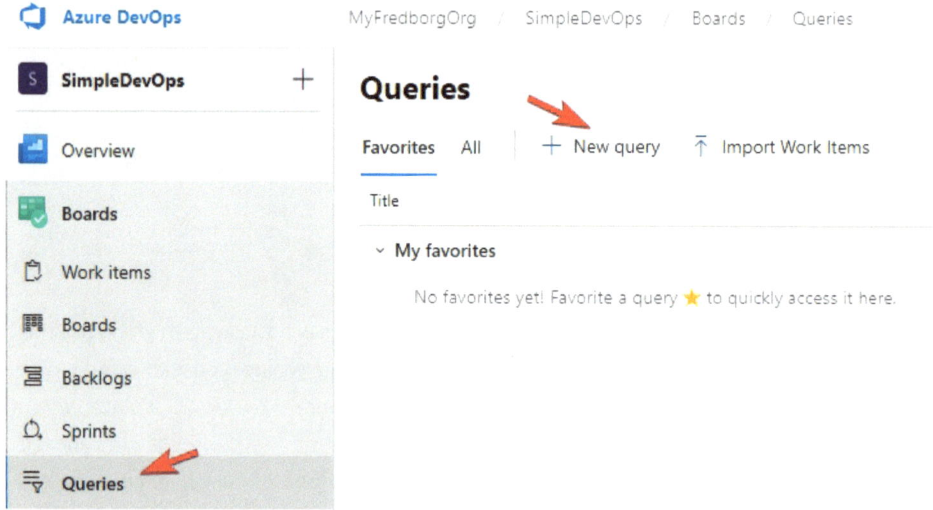

Creating queries is one of those things that are easy to learn but hard to master, it is simple to get started because everything is done through a user interface, so no need to learn any new querying language.

You can also query across all projects, which is very useful if you are part of many projects, and you wish to get an overview of what needs to be done.

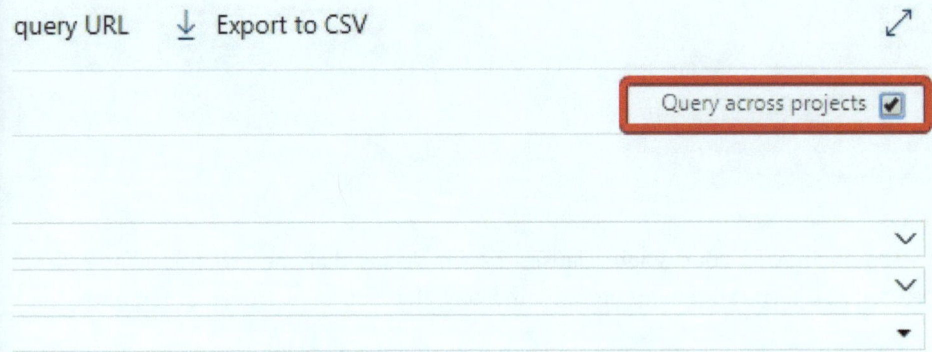

Once you have created a query that you find useful, you can save your query and add it to your dashboards or share it with other people.

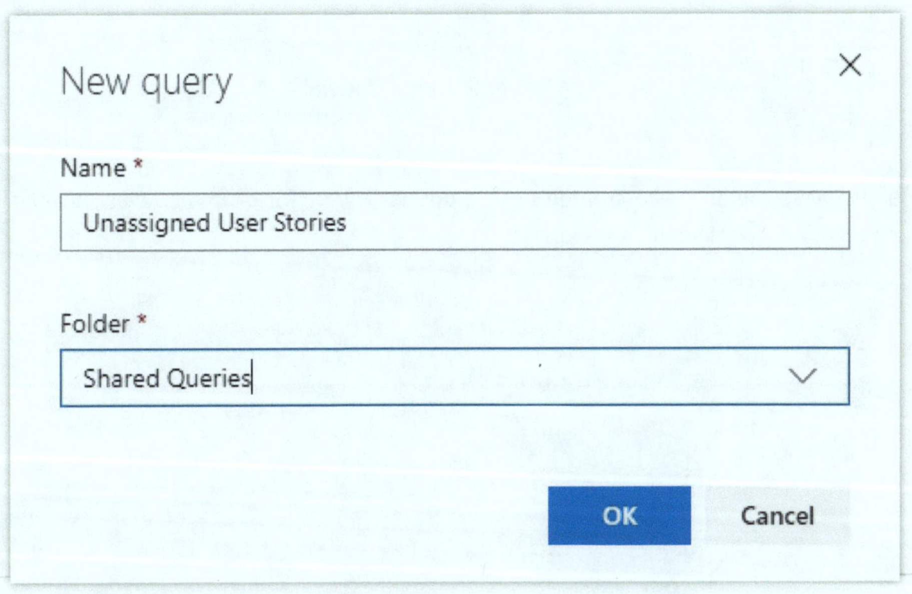

Like I wrote earlier, then it is straightforward to get started, but do not be fooled by the simplicity because you can create very complex quires.

You can also group your where clauses, which means that the group clauses will be executed as a single statement, in the same way, that you know from mathematics.

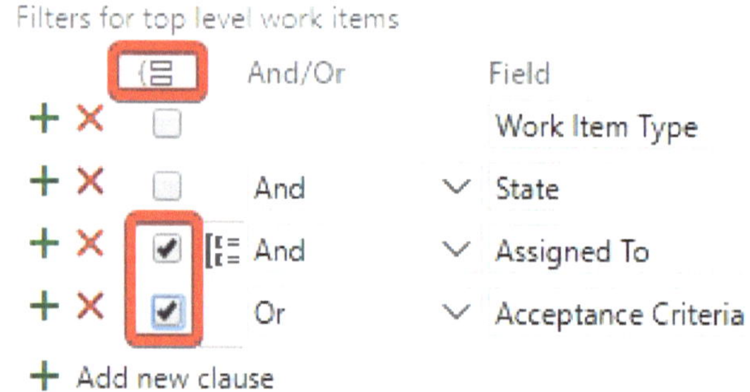

You also have the ability to created nested queries if you, for example, want to get all the work items for all your user stories.

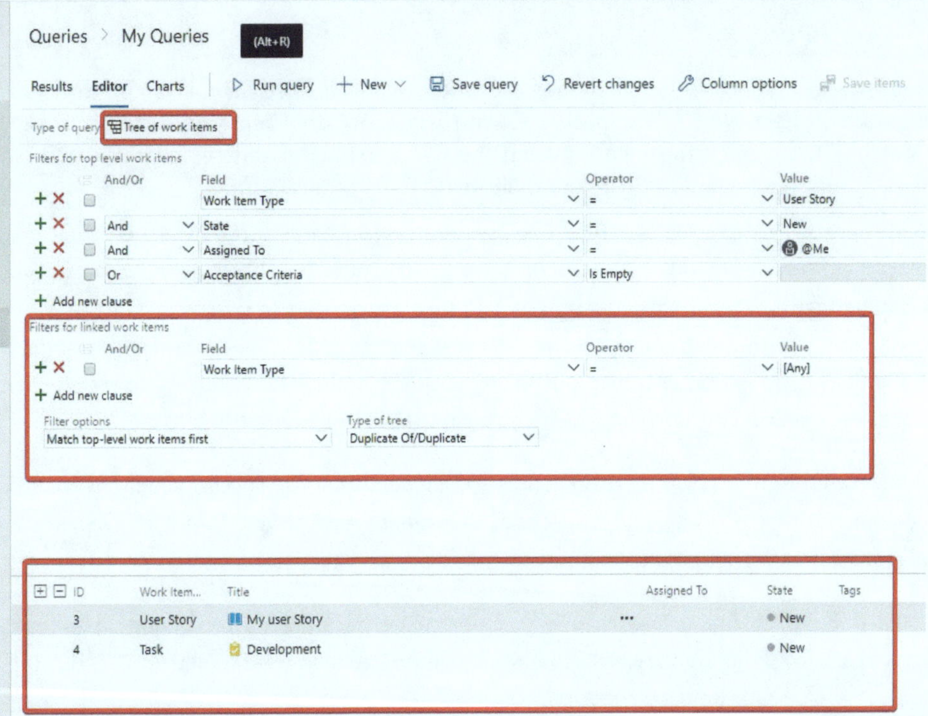

For a more visual overview, you can also create a chart based on your query by clicking the charts and choosing new chart and simply selecting which type of chart that you want; this chart can also be added to your dashboards.

As you can see, you can pretty much build your quires in any way that you want. Another great thing about queries is that you can access them through Azure DevOps REST API, meaning that you can view the result in any third-party system such as PowerBI, once again improving the transparency for your projects.

SUMMARY

To summarize, Azure DevOps provides a set of potent tools to let you run your projects in any way that your wish, that being using sprints or Kanban, and by using quires, you can create views to give you the overview that any of your team members might need.

Repository or Repos for short. Repos are where you will store all your code, when you create a project, you can choose between using GIT and Team Foundation Version Control (TFVC), the difference between the two versions of source control is that GIT runs distributed while TFVC runs centralized.

Distributed: This means that everyone has source control running locally on their own machines, which means that you develop locally, this has both its advantages and disadvantages. One of the advantages to using distributed is that you can break you code locally without breaking the rest of the team's code. The main disadvantage to using distrusted is that you will most likely at some point end up having to merge your code, because two or more people try to push the same code to the master branch.

Centralized: In this setup all code is only running on a central server, which means that you must check out and check in code, this means that if you forget to check in an object no one else can make changes to your object.

Most people will use GIT since it is the most widely supported technology. I will only look at using GIT going forward, however I will not go into how to set up GIT, but only look at what Azure DevOps supports.

MULTI REPOS

You can create as many repositories as you need, giving you an effortless way to separate your code, all projects are created with a default repo, to create a new one you can go to Repos and click the repo name at the top.

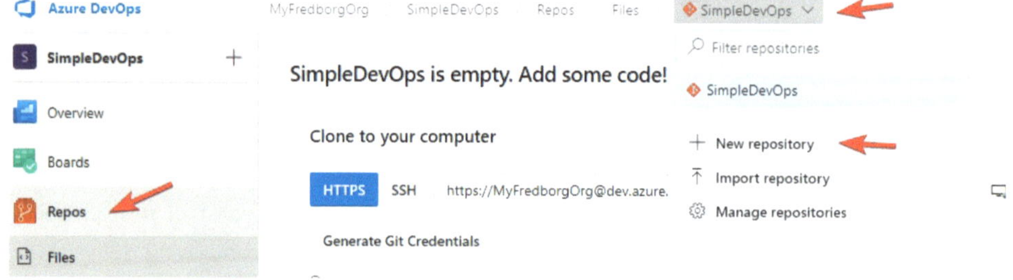

To clone your repo to your local pc you can copy the URL which you find by clicking the clone button.

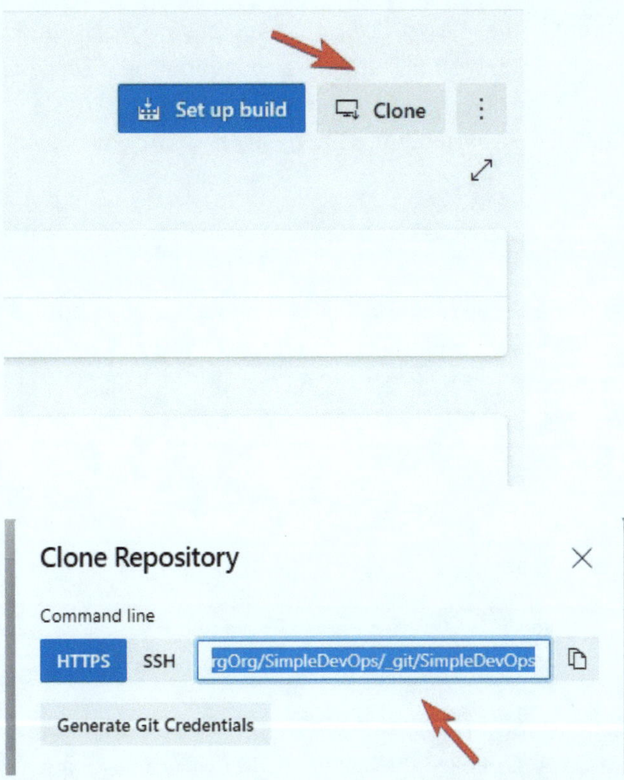

You also have the ability to generate Git Credentials, these can be used if you wish someone to access your repo, but you do not want them to have a full user.

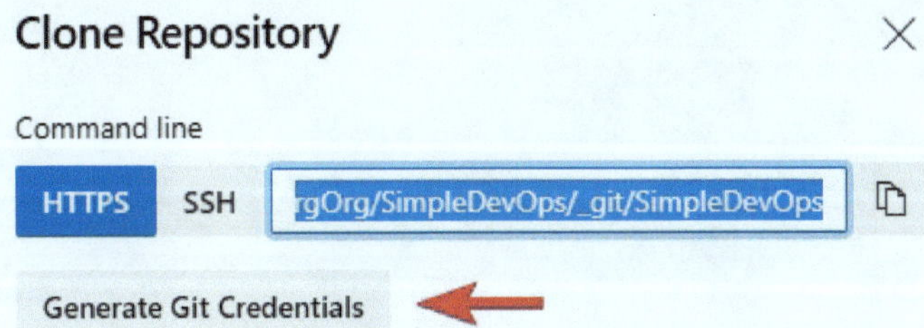

You can create and delete branches by going to the branch's menu item. When you create a new branch, it will be based on you master branch. You should always start all your tasks by creating a new branch, the reason being that you should never work directly in the master / main branch. If you wish to learn more about branches I suggest that you look at https://git-scm.com/book/en/v2/Git-Branching-Branches-in-a-Nutshell like I mentioned earlier then I will not cover how to use GIT, only how GIT works with Azure DevOps.

PULL REQUESTS

This is where you can create and manage pull requests. Pull requests are used to ensure code review of all code that is added to your master / main branch. You can create a new pull in two ways but they both work in the same way, the first you will create a pull request based on your active branches and the other you create a pull request based on any branch.

Once you choose one of the actions you can choose your branch at the top, choose which branch you wish to pull into. You also have the ability to add a title, a description, and which people you wish to review your code, and lastly you can tag the pull request with a work item meaning that you will link the code to a work item, and this will also close your work item.

TIPS GIT WITH DEVOPS

When you create your GIT commands you have some cool options to affect your work items. If you write #workitemid it will add the code to your work item. For example, *#3 added new file*

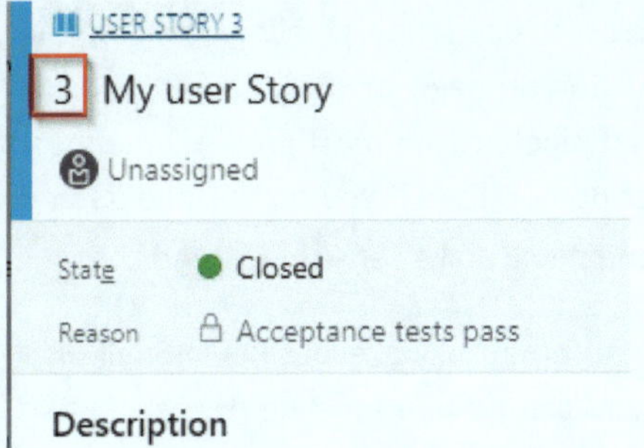

This will link your commit with the work item 3. if you write Fix in the commit it will set your work item to done. For example, *Fix #3 added new file*

Using the above commands will let you work with your work items from your development environment without having to log in to Azure Dev Ops.

SUMMARY

Azure DevOps gives you all the tools that you will need to add your code to source control, and for those of you that already are using some sort of source control then everything should work as you are used to, Microsoft has not tried to reinvent anything in their repository which is actually a good thing ☐.

Pipelines are one of the most important things in DevOps, the reason being that if you want to be able to successfully implement CI/CD you must be able to automatically test and deploy your code. To accomplish this Microsoft has made pipelines available in Azure DevOps, but what are pipelines and what do you need to setup to get started? Before we get started, I just want to warn you that pipelines are most properly the most complicated part of Azure DevOps, so do not get demoralized if you do not understand everything the first time around, just keep at it and it will make sense in the end ☐.

In a nutshell then pipelines are a way for you to automatically execute PowerShell on a server. So, anything you can do in PowerShell you can do in a pipeline, there are two types of pipelines, you have a build pipeline which is used to build and test your code, and when executed should result in a build artifact, which is a compiled or release ready version of your code. Next you have the release pipeline which is used to release your artifacts to both testing and production. But before we get into creating the pipelines, let us look at what you need to get everything setup.

ENVIRONMENTS

Using environments allows you to organize your resources, which you can target in your pipelines, when you create a new environment you have the choice to create, a blank environment, where you will add your resources later, to create it with a Kubernetes namespace or with a virtual machine.

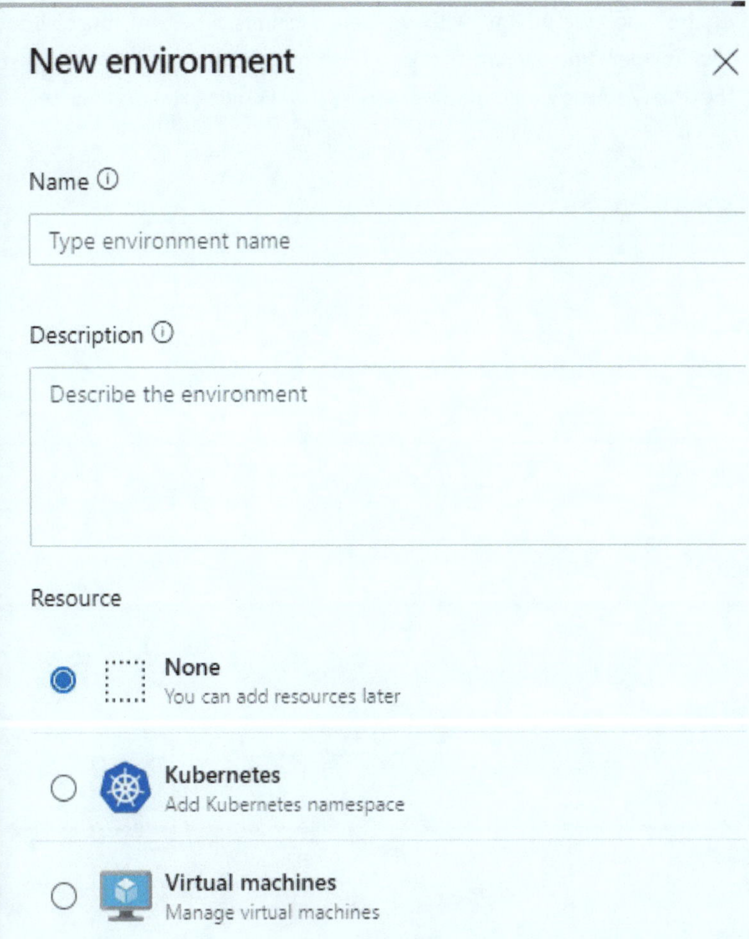

Kubernetes: Is a way to run a containerized environment, and in many cases the best choice when it comes to CI/CD because it runs without much setup, however it also requires you to understand how containers work.

Virtual machine: This could be a server anywhere as long as it has an internet connection, if you choose this option you will be presented with a PowerShell script that you can run on your server which will install an azure agent, allowing your pipelines to execute code on your remote server.

For the purpose of this book we will go with Virtual machines, first you must choose your provider and what operating system that you wish to run you agent on, and lastly you will be given the ability to copy a PowerShell script, that you can run on your server:

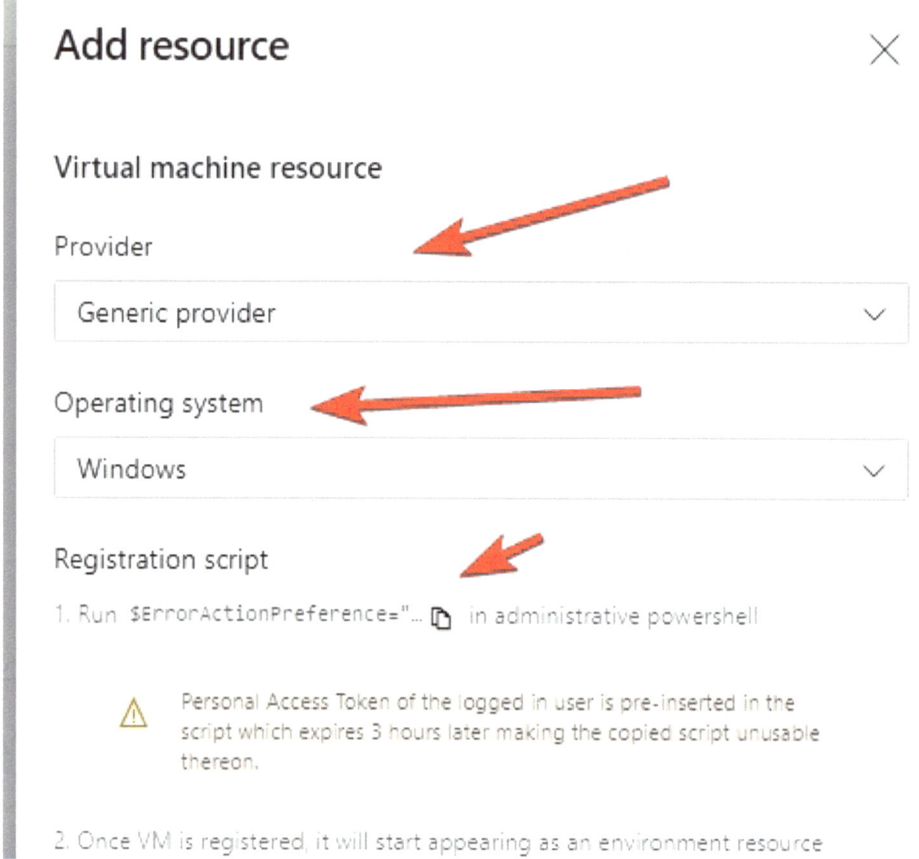

On you server start a PowerShell prompt as administrator (not an ISE) and paste your PowerShell script into the prompt and run it:

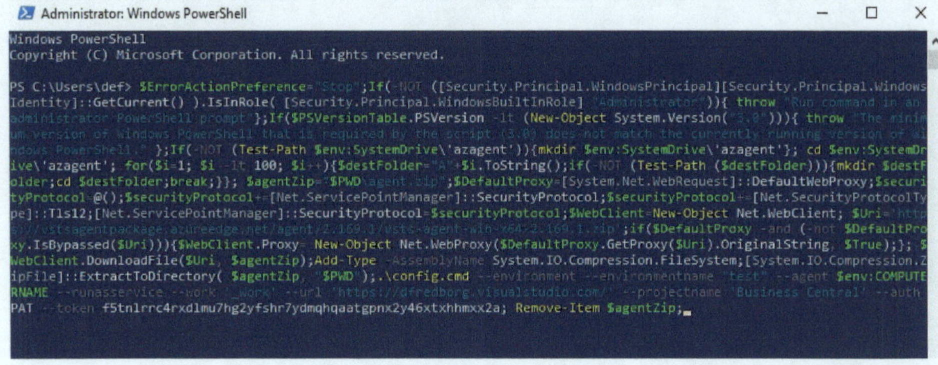

The script will take some time to execute because it must first download the Azure agent so be patient if it looks like it is stuck on the following screen then press enter:

You should then be guided through the setup process:

```
Mode                LastWriteTime         Length Name
----                -------------         ------ ----
d-----       6/10/2020    9:39 AM                A1


    _____                        _____  _                  _  _
   /  _  \  ____ _____ _________ |  _  \(_) _ __   ___ _  (_)| | __   ___  ___
  /  /_\  \/_  // | | |\_  __ \  | |_) || || '_ \ / _ \ | || || |/ /  / _ \/ __|
 /    |    \/  /\  |_|  | | \/  |  __/ | || |_) |  __/ | || ||   <  |  __/\__ \
 \____|__  /_____/\____/ |_|    |_|    |_|| .__/ \___| |_||_||_|\_\  \___||___/
         \/                               |_|

        agent v2.169.1                    |_|                (commit ac1c169)


>> Connect:

Connecting to server ...

>> Register Agent:

Scanning for tool capabilities.
Connecting to the server.
Enter Environment Virtual Machine resource tags? (Y/N) (press enter for N) > _
```

For the propose of this book I will just leave everything default, and at last you should
see something like this:

```
>> Connect:

Connecting to server ...

>> Register Agent:

Scanning for tool capabilities.
Connecting to the server.
Enter Environment Virtual Machine resource tags? (Y/N) (press enter for N) >
Successfully added the agent
Testing agent connection.
2020-06-10 09:44:00Z: Settings Saved.
Enter User account to use for the service (press enter for NT AUTHORITY\SYSTEM) >
Error reported in diagnostic logs. Please examine the log for more details.
    - C:\azagent\A1\_diag\Agent_20200610-093952-utc.log
Granting file permissions to 'NT AUTHORITY\SYSTEM'.
Service vstsagent.dfredborg..mycicd successfully installed
Service vstsagent.dfredborg..mycicd successfully set recovery option
Service vstsagent.dfredborg..mycicd successfully set to delayed auto start
Service vstsagent.dfredborg..mycicd successfully configured
Service vstsagent.dfredborg..mycicd started successfully


PS C:\azagent\A1> _
```

If you now go back to your Azure DevOps, you should see that your server has been
added as a resource:

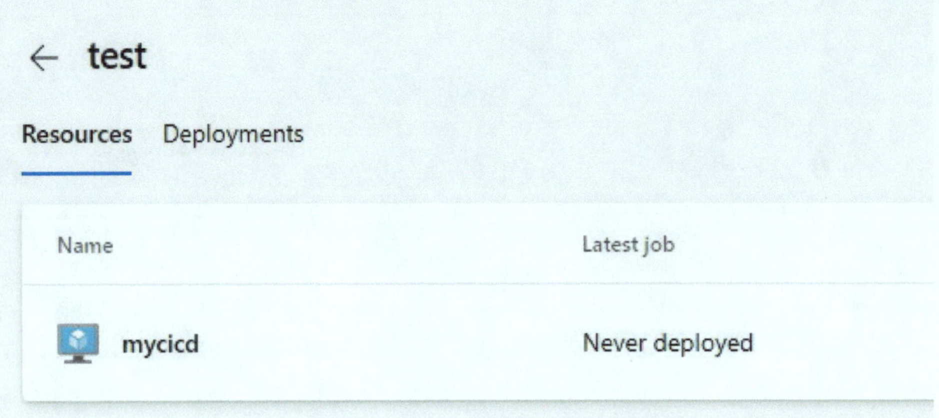

So next time you target your environment it will be deployed on your server. And that is pretty much everything you need to create your pipelines but let us first take a look at what other tools you have available.

Library: This is a place where you have the ability to create variables that you wish to share across your pipelines. This is good place to store your user credentials, and remember to mark your password as secret, and if you are working with containers you could also store your image name here:

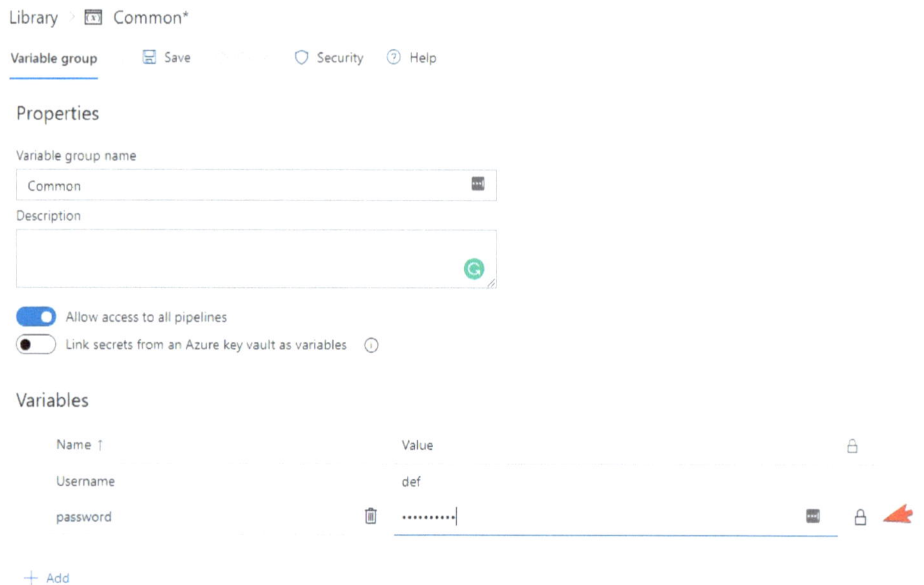

You can also add secure files to your library, so you do not have to add them to your repository.

Now let us create our pipeline ☐ so go to pipeline and choose create pipeline:

For this example, I have created a new repository called mypipeline where I have added a file called createfile.ps1 with the PowerShell code new-item -Path C:\newfile.txt

Once you click the Create Pipeline you will be asked to choose where your code is placed in my example I will choose Azure Repos Glt, but as you can see then one of the great things about Azure DevOps is that it does not force you to use their source control, but you are allowed to integrate to other systems.

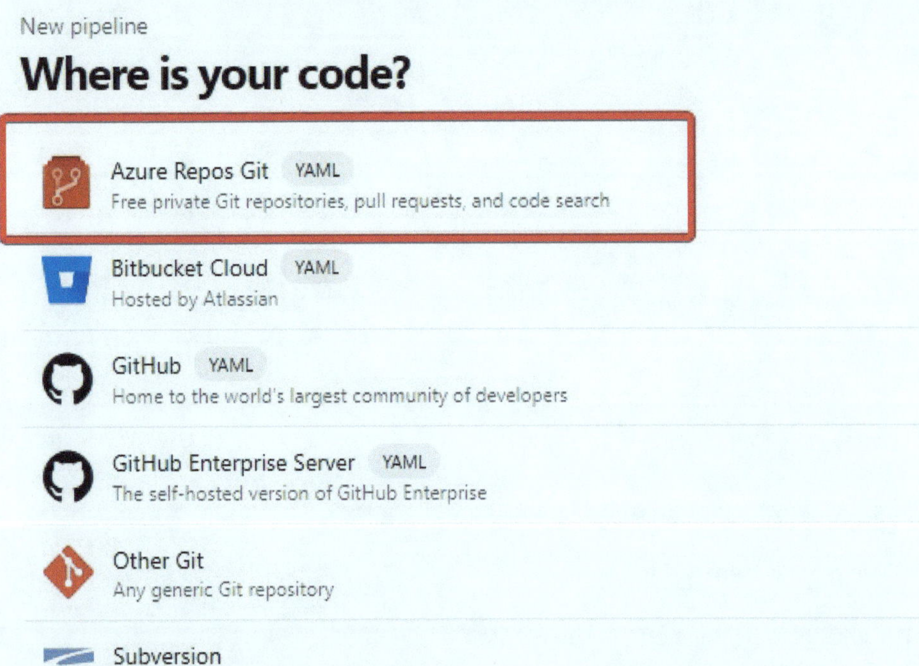

Next I will choose my repository, and choose the starter pipeline, which will generate some XAML code for you:

```yaml
1   # Starter pipeline
2   # Start with a minimal pipeline that you can customize to build and deploy your code.
3   # Add steps that build, run tests, deploy, and more:
4   # https://aka.ms/yaml
5
6   trigger:
7   - master
8
9   pool:
10    vmImage: 'ubuntu-latest'
11
12  steps:
13  - script: echo Hello, world!
14    displayName: 'Run a one-line script'
15
16  - script: |
17      echo Add other tasks to build, test, and deploy your project.
18      echo See https://aka.ms/yaml
19    displayName: 'Run a multi-line script'
20
```

1) Defines what you trigger your pipeline

2) Defines which pool you which to use and which image.

3) Defines your steps

4) What should be done on the current step

Now let us try to change our pipeline so that it executes on our server:

```yaml
1
2  trigger:
3  - master
4
5  stages:
6  - stage: deploy
7    jobs:
8    - deployment: MyDeploymentGroup
9      displayName: deploy PowerShell
10
11     environment:
12       name: Test
13       resourceName: mycicd
14       resourceType: VirtualMachine
15     strategy:
16       runOnce:
17         deploy:
18           steps:
                Settings
19           - task: PowerShell@2
20             inputs:
21               targetType: 'inline'
22               script: 'new-item -Path C:\newfile.txt'
23
24
25  |
```

The environment is where you define where your code should be executed, and the next thing that happens is that it executes an inline PowerShell script on our agent, which in this case just creates a blank text file in the root of our C drive, but it could do anything, once you save and run your pipeline you might be met with a permission warning:

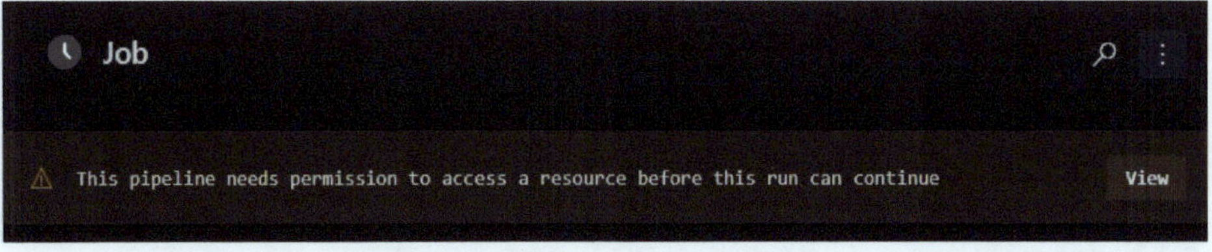

You must click view and permit

And your pipeline should run with success

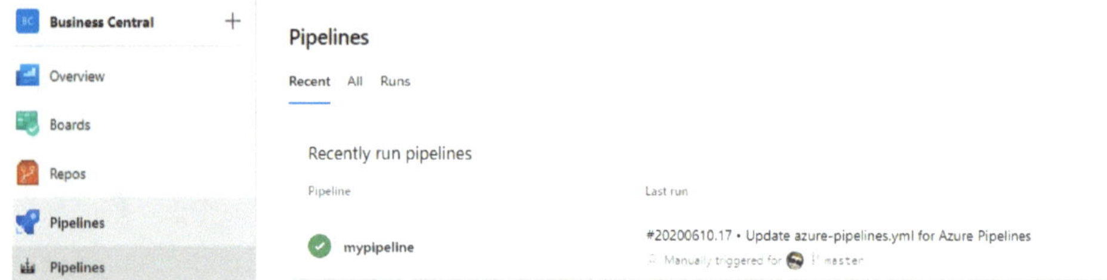

If you go to Environments and go to your environment, you will also be able to see which jobs has run on which resources.

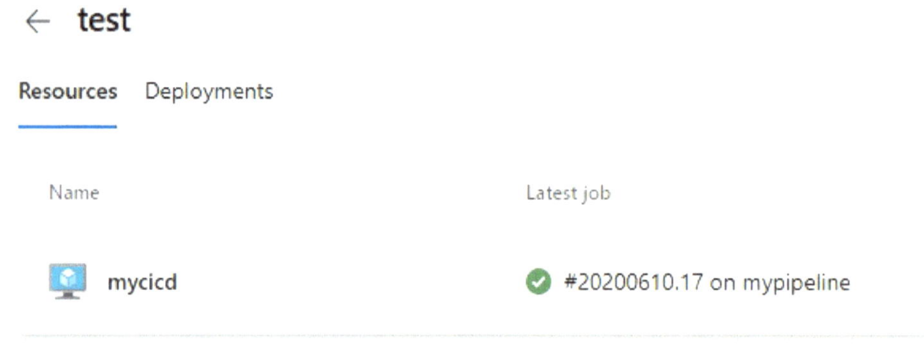

This is very useful because it will easily let you see if all your builds are running as expected. You can do a lot of things with your pipelines and to get some help you should try to look at the assistant which will give you snippets to help you implement different tasks. To view the assistant, go to your pipelines and click edit.

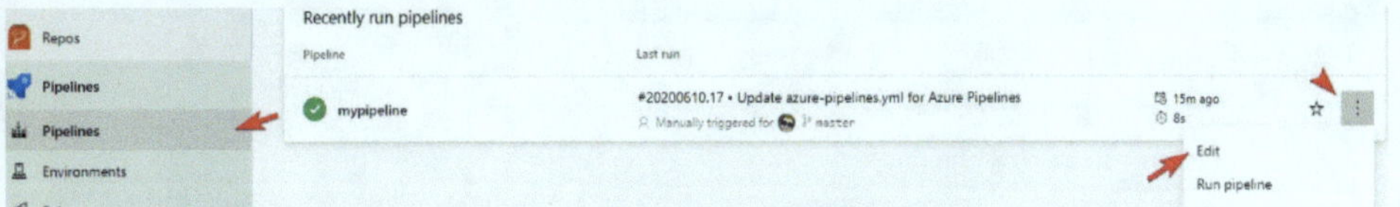

And choose Show assistant

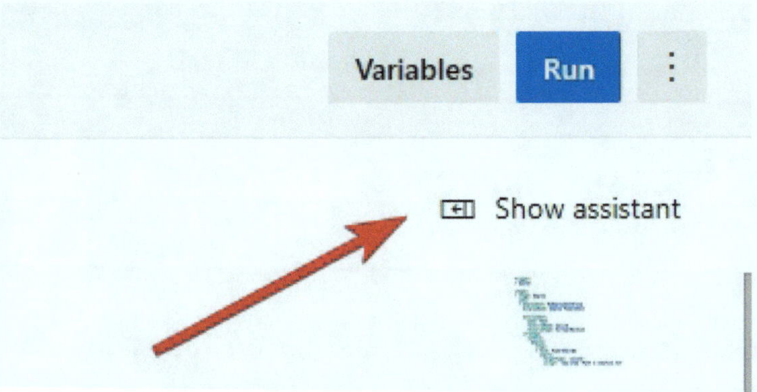

And then type what you want to achieve, and a list of possibilities will appear

Just click on one of the tasks, fill out the fields and choose add, and you have created a new task in your pipeline.

SUMMARY

Pipelines are very powerful tool, but can also be very complicated, and unfortunately since pipelines are very unique from project to project, it would be too complex to go into too much detail in this book, as pipelines should be a book on it's own, but I hope that this gave you some inspiration on how to get started.

Test plans is one of those features that you do not get out of the box, however it is possible to enable a 30 day trial to see if it is something for you, to enable the trial go to your Organization settings, go to billing and start trial.

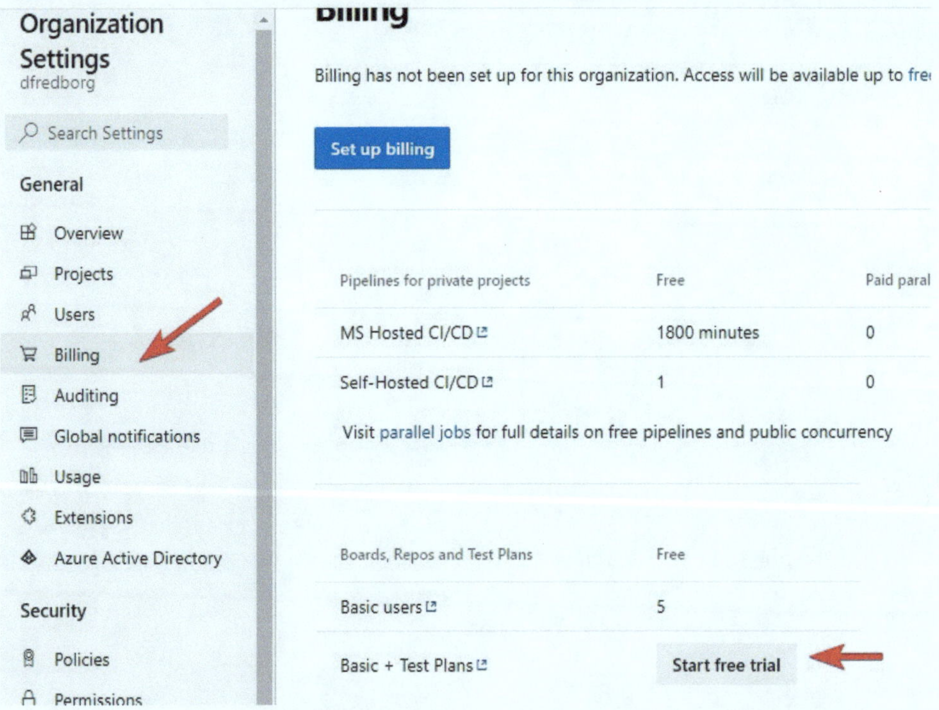

You should now be able to see the following menu items in your project

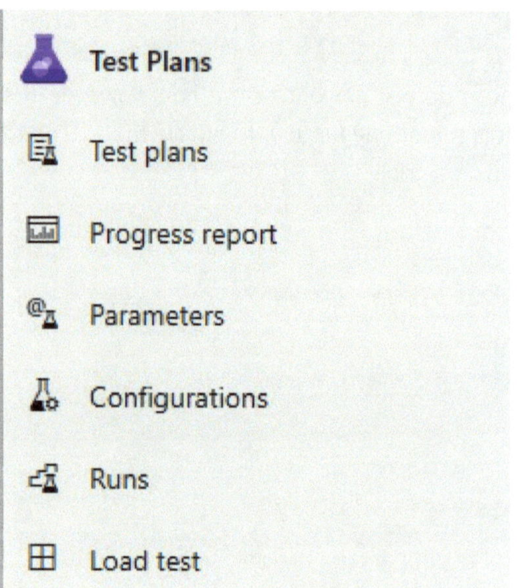

So let us just take them from the top.

TEST PLANS

You have the ability to create a new test plan by going to test plan and clicking New Test Plan.

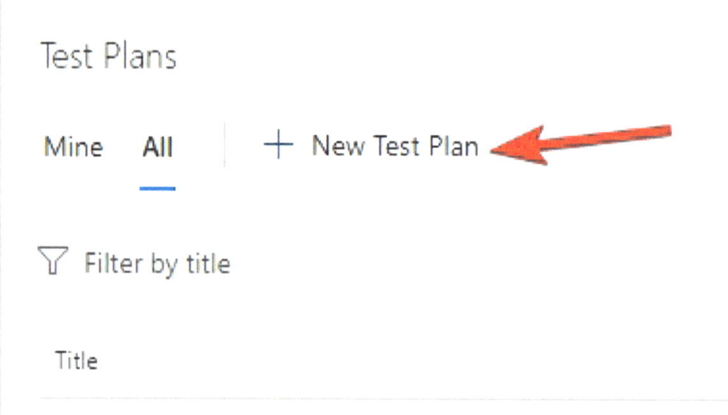

You must then give it a name and choose which Iteration it should be bound to.

Next you can start creating your test cases or add any existing test cases to your test plan. A test case is built up in steps, where each step has an action which might result in an expected result, and you can add an attachment.

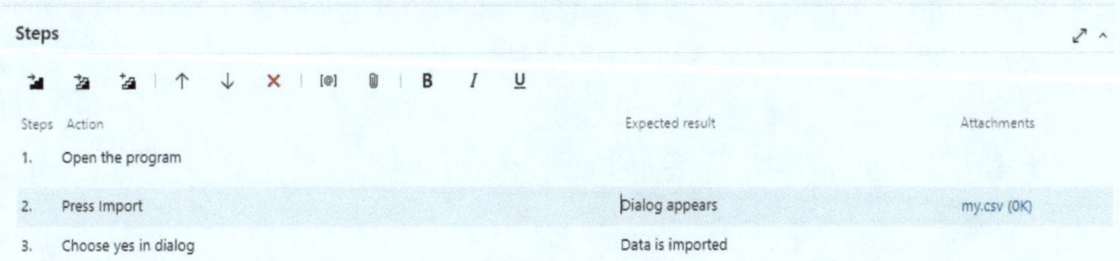

You also have the ability to add a small summary of what your test case is trying to test.

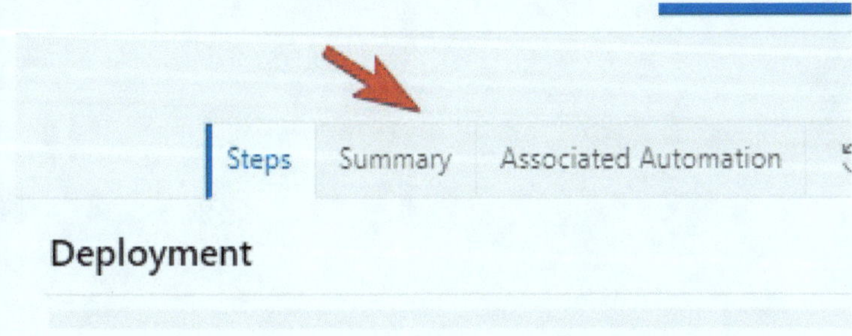

Deployment

Once you have created your Test Case, your testers can then test your test cases and mark them according to the outcome.

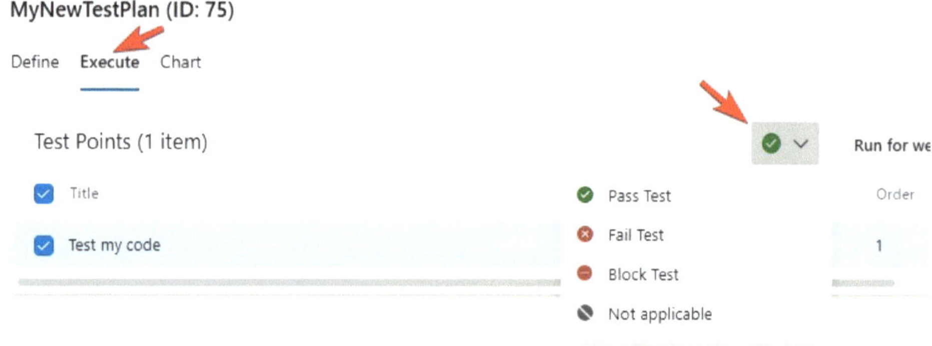

PROGRESS REPORT

Here you can get an overview of the status of your project, showing you if your tests are passing or failing.

PARAMETERS

Here you can create a collection of values that you wish to use in your Test Cases, you could for example create a parameter group called Colors and add some colors to it.

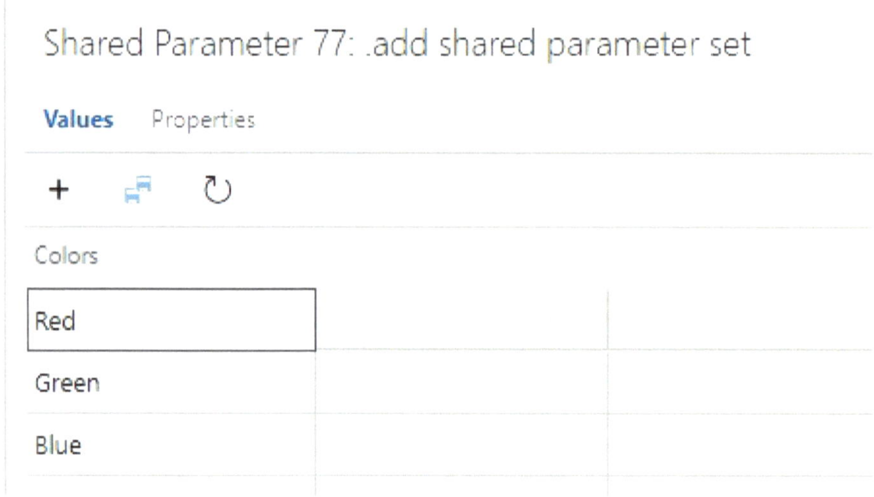

You can then add them to your test case by using @Colors.

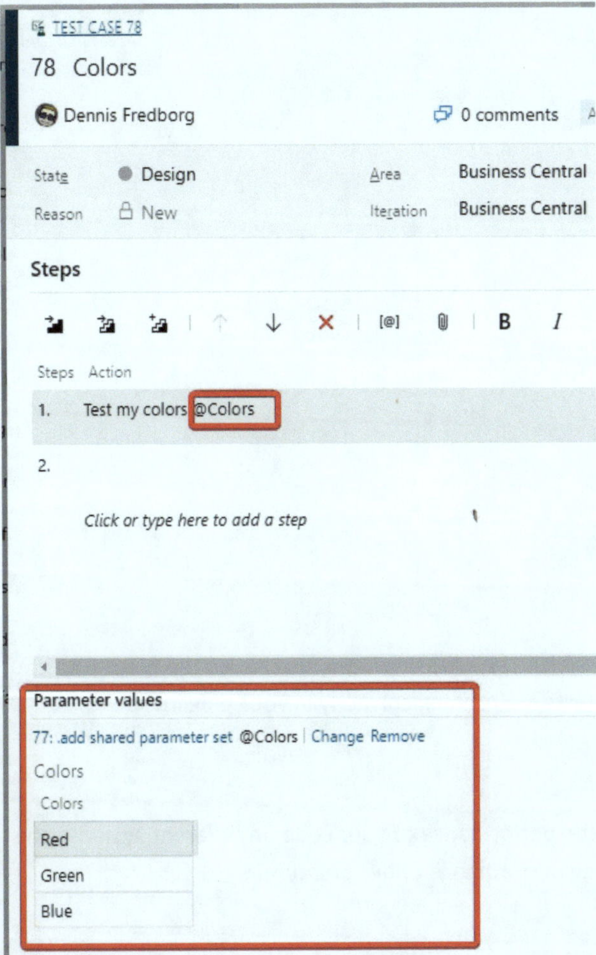

You can also add local parameters to your test cases, the idea behind parameters is to ensure that your test cases are executed the correct way.

CONFIGURATIONS

Here you can store the configurations, on which you wish to test your code, this is a tool to help the old question, what system are you running? Because is works fine on my PC.

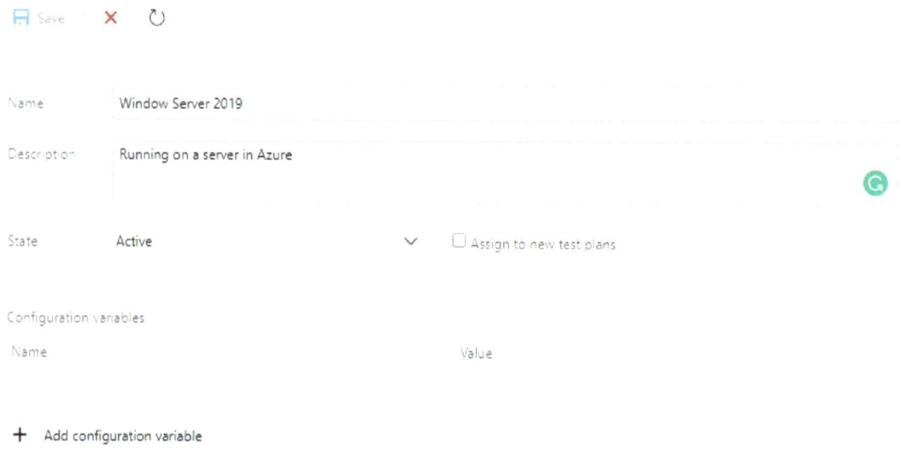

RUNS

Here you have the ability to view which tests has been run, this is also the place that you would be able to see if your unit tests are running correctly in your pipelines.

LOAD TEST

Here you have the ability to test the performance of your code on different systems, this is great place to see how your code performance under pressure.

TEST AND FEED BACK

If your system is running in a browser, Microsoft has created a great tool for your customers to be able to report bugs and or features. All you must do is install the chrome add in called Test & Feedback

 chrome webshop

Start > Udvidelser > Test & Feedback

Test & Feedback

Fra: Microsoft Corporation

★★★★☆ 159 | **Produktivitet** | 👤 90.000+ brugere

Once this is installed you must then setup the plugin to access your Azure DevOps'

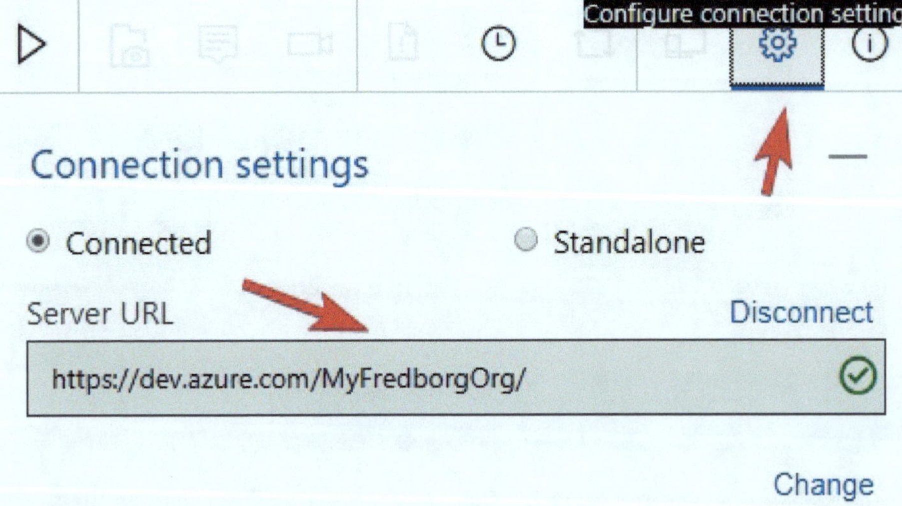

Once that is setup you can press the play button, which will give you a set of tools to create a bug or a task directly from your own web page. In the below example I have taken a screenshot, using the plugin and created a bug with the name new bug.

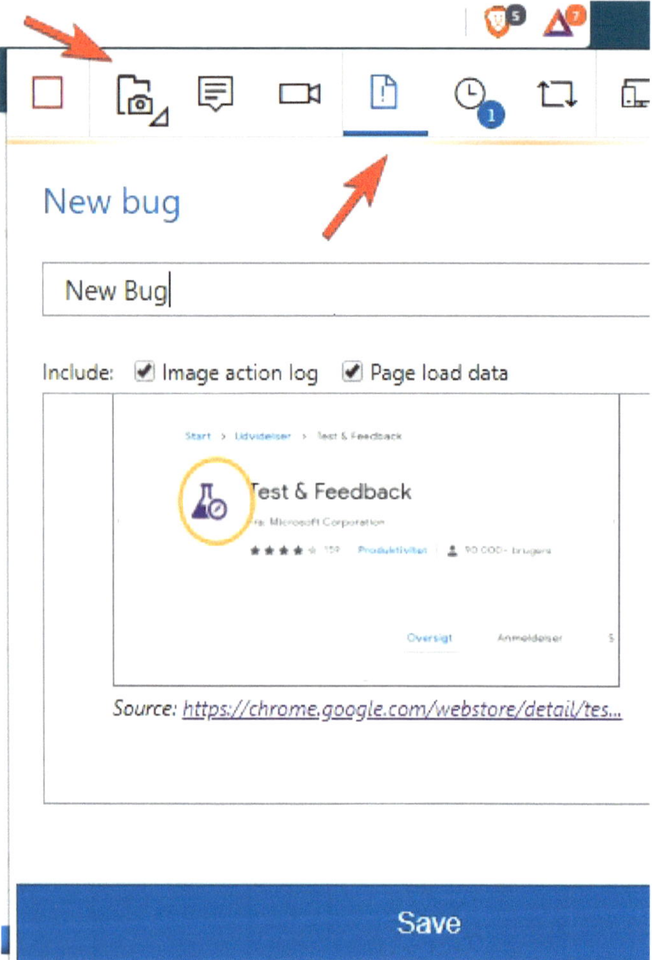

When I then go back to my Azure DevOps I now have a new bug with all the system information.

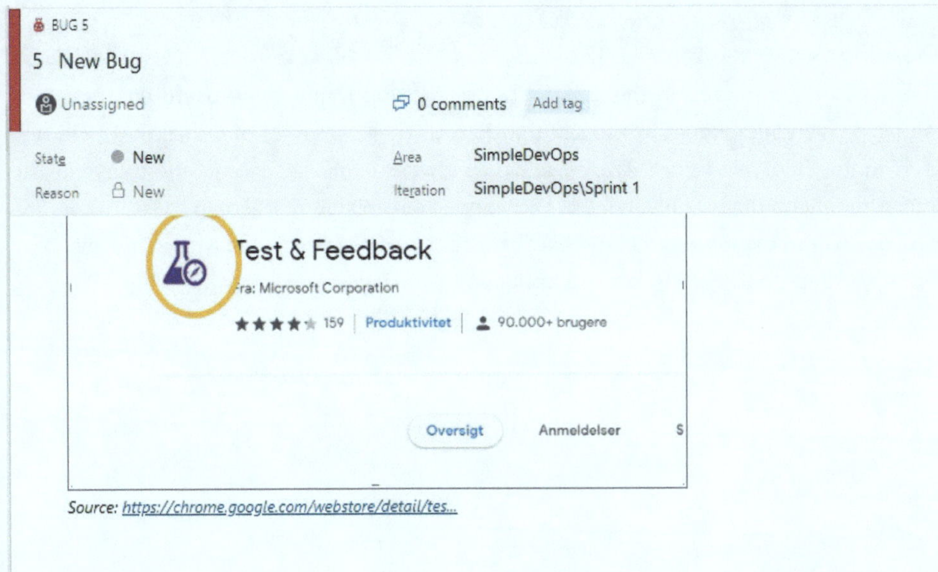

Source: _https://chrome.google.com/webstore/detail/tes..._

System Info

Browser - Name	Google Chrome 81
Browser - Language	en-US
Browser - Height	960
Browser - Width	1551
Browser - UserAgent	Mozilla/5.0 (Windows NT 10.0; Win64; x64) AppleWebKit/537.36 (KHTML, like Gecko) Chrome/81.0.4044.138 Safari/537.36
OS - Name	Windows NT 10.0; Win64; x64
OS - Architecture	x86_64
OS - ProcessorModel	Intel(R) Core(TM) i7-8650U CPU @ 1.90GHz
OS - NumberOfProcessors	8
Memory - Available	3435069440

Could it be any easier ☐ and you can also record your screen and add a video, so no more reporting bugs with little to no information.

SUMMARY

Testing is one of those things that we all talk about, but only a very few of us do it, with Azure DevOps you are given the ability to create systematic tests, and with their chrome plugin, reporting bugs could not be easier.

That is all I have for you in this book, I hope that you found some useful information. Before I leave you, I would like to say that I know there are a lot of things that I did not cover in this book, and since Azure DevOps is always evolving some of the things might unfortunately no longer be valid. But I still hope that this book will help to ignite the fire and your will to explorer the many excellent features of Microsoft's Azure DevOps. And as always keep up the will to keep learning and evolving.

* 9 7 9 8 7 2 2 8 9 2 6 9 0 *